◆ In Celebration of ◆

_____

A special book
for your
special day!

_____

Place & Date

Name

Wishes

Picture of the day

Name

Wishes

Picture of the day

Name

Wishes

Picture of the day

Name

Wishes

Picture of the day

Name

Wishes

Picture of the day

Name

Wishes

Picture of the day

Name

Wishes

Picture of the day

Name

Wishes

Picture of the day

Name

Wishes

Picture of the day

Name

Wishes

Picture of the day

Name

Wishes

Picture of the day

Name

Wishes

Picture of the day

Name

Wishes

Picture of the day

Name

Wishes

Picture of the day

Name

Wishes

Picture of the day

Name

Wishes

Picture of the day

Name

Wishes

Picture of the day

Name

Wishes

Picture of the day

Name

Wishes

Picture of the day

Name

Wishes

Picture of the day

Name

Wishes

Picture of the day

Name

Wishes

Picture of the day

Name

Wishes

Picture of the day

Name

Wishes

Picture of the day

Name

Wishes

Picture of the day

Name

Wishes

Picture of the day

Name

Wishes

Picture of the day

Name

Wishes

Picture of the day

Name

Wishes

Picture of the day

Made in the USA
Coppell, TX
15 November 2024

40312020R00035